washington DC

P9-AOU-833

Legend

NumbersAlive! Stops	
Places You Might Want to See	
Circulator Routes	
Hospital	
M Metro	
Metro Exit	
Museum / Memorial / Monument	
Point Of Interest	
2 Theatre	
University	

Mt Vernon Sq-7th St/Convention Center

New York Ave-Florida Ave-Gallaudet U

Walter E. Washington Convention Center

L St NW Historic

National Portrait Gallery

Chinatown
Gallery Place-Chinatown
Friendship Arch

American Art Museum
Verizon Center

Ford's Theatre

Judiciary Square

National Building Museum

National Guard Museum

Union Station
Columbus Circle

Postal Museum

National Archives
Archives Navy Memorial-Penn

Newseum

NGA Sculpture Gallery

National Gallery of Art East

US Capitol & Visitor Center

United States Supreme Court
Folger Shakespeare Library

Capitol Hill
Library of Congress Jefferson Building

Smithsonian Castle
African Art and Industries Museum
Hirshhorn Museum

Jefferson Dr, SW
National Air and Space Museum

National Museum of The American Indian

US Botanic Garden

L'Enfant Plaza

Federal Center SW

Capitol South

Eastern Market

Southeast Fwy

Southeast Fwy

Waterfront/SEU

Navy Yard

Southwest/Waterfront

Nationals Park

Yards Park

Anacostia River

Dr. Rebecca Klemm is the founder and Executive Director of NumbersAlive! She is an experienced educator who has taught statistics and mathematics at the middle-school, high-school, and university levels. To address the urgent need to engage young people and caring adults in a friendly approach to improve numerical literacy, she became "The Numbers Lady" and created Zero the Hero and Team Ten (fun, flexible, and friendly animated number characters 0–9).

Dr. Klemm's program uses the arts and real-world adventures to encourage children to observe and speak about numbers in their own environments. It establishes a solid knowledge foundation for STEM (science, technology, engineering, and mathematics) academic subjects.

Team Ten, led by Zero the Hero, accompanies Dr. Klemm and pre-K through Grade 5 children on innovative, interpersonal, and interactive global education quests. They discover numerical applications and develop concepts of the scientific method. The learning adventure begins in Washington, DC!

Message from The Numbers Lady

Welcome to Washington, DC, the capital city of the United States of America!

You are about to begin an educational quest with the friendly number characters of Team Ten, led by Zero the Hero. Team Ten will show you around the city and share facts about numbers and history. As Team Ten members find and describe their favorite locations, you will learn how numbers are relevant in everyday life.

Each page of your book includes an informative verse, a secret question—posed by a member of Team Ten—and an answer, plus a factoid about the DC location. More fun facts about each location are included in the back of the book, along with a short guide for parents, teachers, and librarians about how to use this educational resource.

I hope you enjoy learning about Washington, DC and the importance of numbers with Team Ten! Please let me know how you like your tour.

Dr. Klemm

Dr. Klemm, The Numbers Lady   TheNumbersLady@numbersalive.org

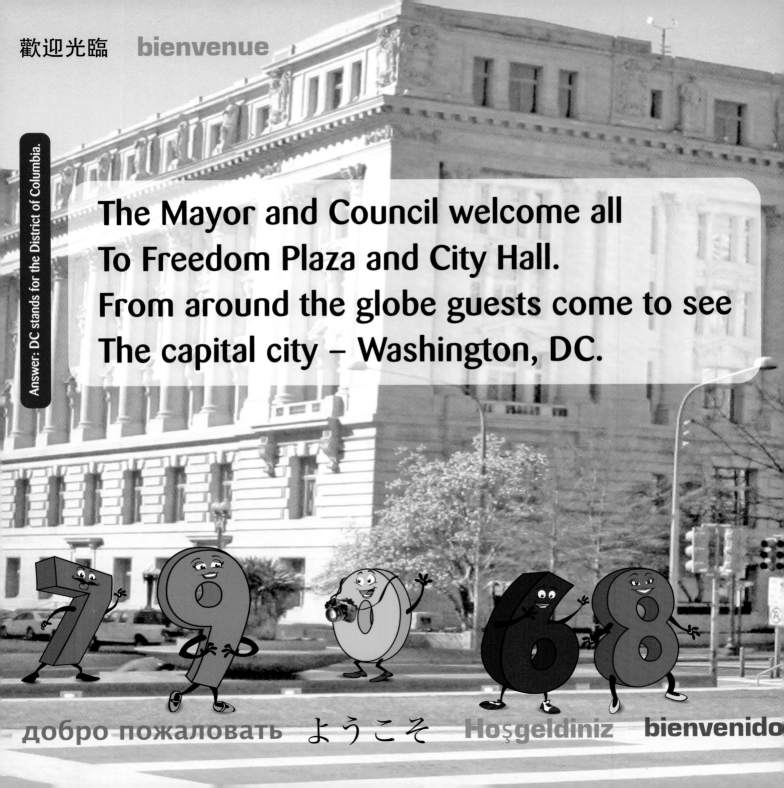

歡迎光臨　bienvenue

The Mayor and Council welcome all
To Freedom Plaza and City Hall.
From around the globe guests come to see
The capital city – Washington, DC.

добро пожаловать　ようこそ　Hoşgeldiniz　bienvenido

We're at the White House; it's looking so fine.
We're proud to be here, Numbers 0 through 9!

Next stop: 1's favorite place ➡

Answer: The president's family, called the "First Family."

555 feet and
5 $^1/_8$ inches

I look like the monument that makes my heart sing.
The 1st President, Washington, refused to be king.

Next stop: 0's favorite place

Factoid: The monument has 1 elevator and 896 steps.

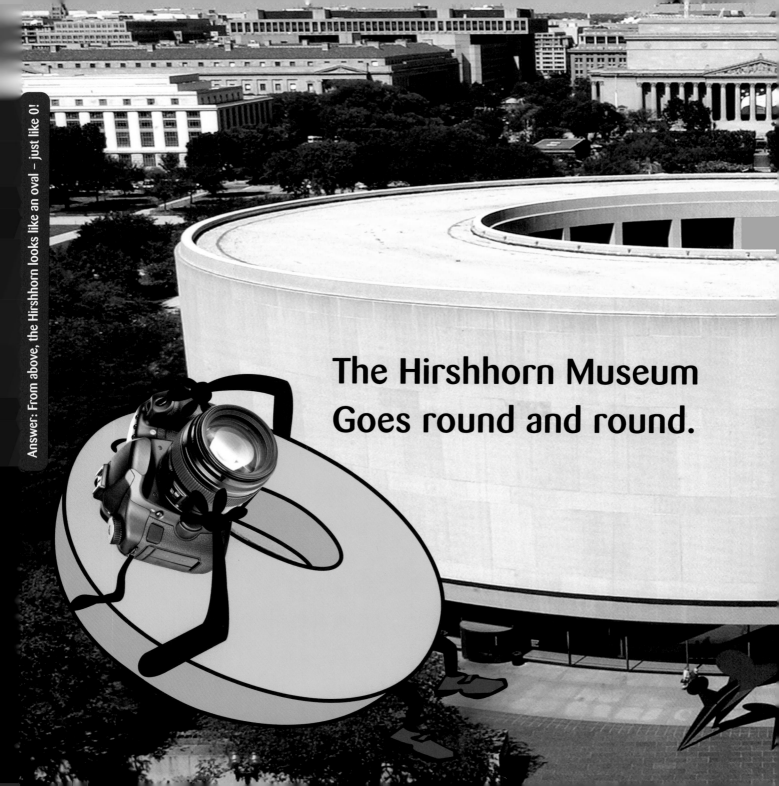

The Hirshhorn Museum
Goes round and round.

Inside and out
Art and sculpture abound.

Why did 0 choose the Hirshhorn as a favorite place?

Factoid: Joseph Hirshhorn's gift to the nation of approximately 6,000 pieces of art in the 1960s established the Hirshhorn Museum and Sculpture Garden.

Next stop: 6's favorite place →

6th and Independence – a fun place to be,
Air & Space has highlights – these 6 you must see.
I'm here in a spacesuit playing tricks.
Yes! You guessed right. I'm the number 6!

INTERSTATE 66

Touch the Moon Rock!

6 ST SW 200

Next stop: 4's favorite place

Lady Liberty tops the Capitol dome.
It's also the place that Congress calls home.
It's where legislators make laws within
And DC's geographic quadrants begin.

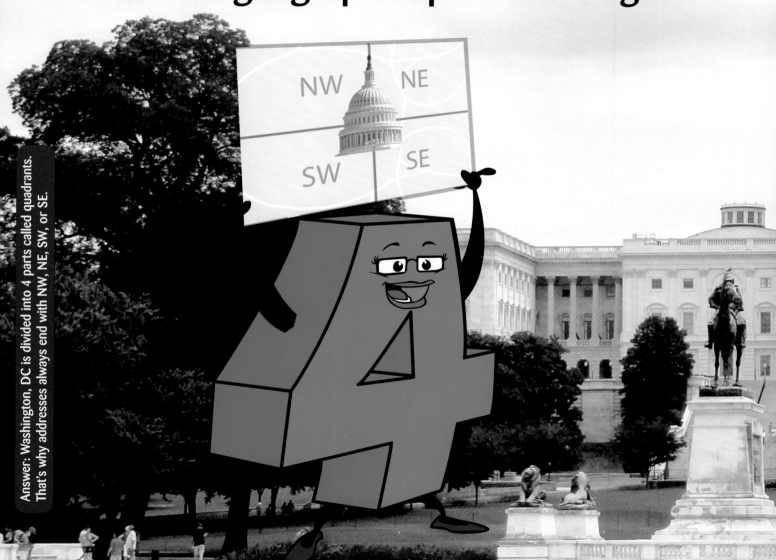

In robes, 9 Supreme Court Justices look grand
As they interpret the laws that guide the land.

Museums and treasures line the "Nation's Backyard,"
With the Capitol and Lincoln standing on guard.

RECYCLE
for a bright future

There's a castle and carousel on the National Mall,
Where we walk and ride bikes and think freedom for all.

If this is the Mall, where are the shops?

Factoid: The National Mall is a 2-mile-long stretch of land between the Capitol and the Lincoln Memorial.

Next stop: Picnic Lunch ➡

Martin Luther King, Jr. was an American son
Who believed in equality for everyone.
Judge people by their actions, he would preach,
As shared in his famous "I Have a Dream" speech.

Where was the "I Have a Dream" speech delivered?

Next stop: Yellow line Metro

Riding the Metro is a fun thing to do.
Wave back at Team Ten as they wave to you.

Answer: The Potomac River.

L'Enfant Plaza

Pentagon

Yellow Line

Next stop: 5's favorite place ➤

ARMY

NAVY

AIR FORCE

MARINES

COAST GUARD

The 5-sided Pentagon is really quite grand.
5 military branches protect US land.

Answer: Yes. A pentagon is a shape with 5 sides. The Pentagon houses the US Department of Defense.

The National Archives' triangle is as pretty as can be.
Inside are historic documents for everyone to see.

Is 3's tricorn hat also a triangle?

Factoid: The 3 most famous documents in the Archives are the Declaration of Independence, the US Constitution, and the US Bill of Rights.

Next stop: 7's favorite place ⟹

Answer: Yes. Tricorn hats were popular during the Revolutionary War, 1775-1783.

At 7th Street the Friendship Arch, a gift from China, stands.
It links Beijing with Washington and celebrates our lands.

Answer: 7, of course!

矗立在第七街的友 谊牌坊是来自中 国的礼物。
它 连接着北京和华盛顿，共同庆贺两国的友谊！

中國城
台山酒家
TAISHAN
How many roofs are on the arch?
Next stop: 8's favorite place

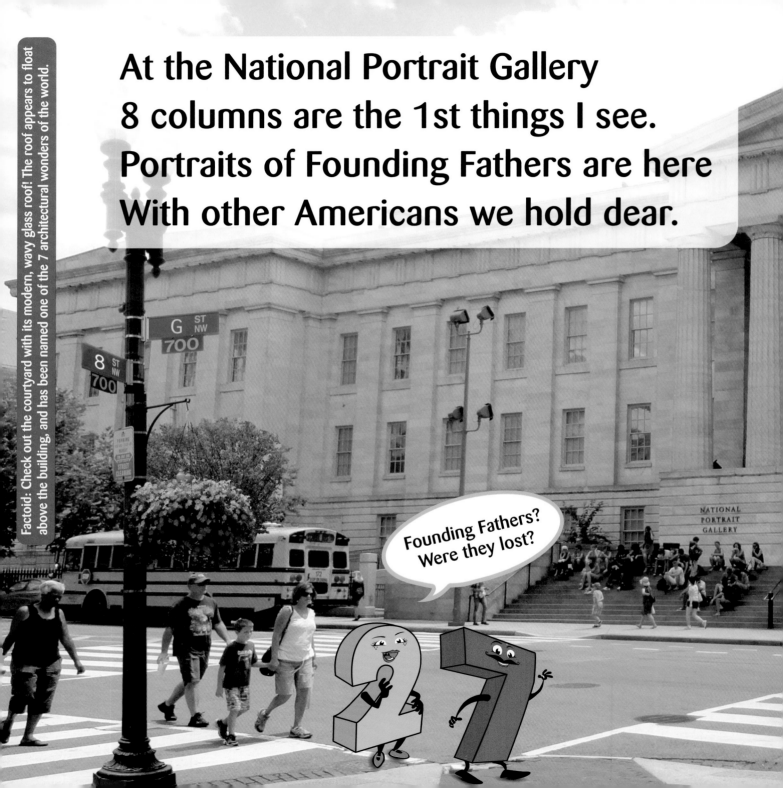

At the National Portrait Gallery
8 columns are the 1st things I see.
Portraits of Founding Fathers are here
With other Americans we hold dear.

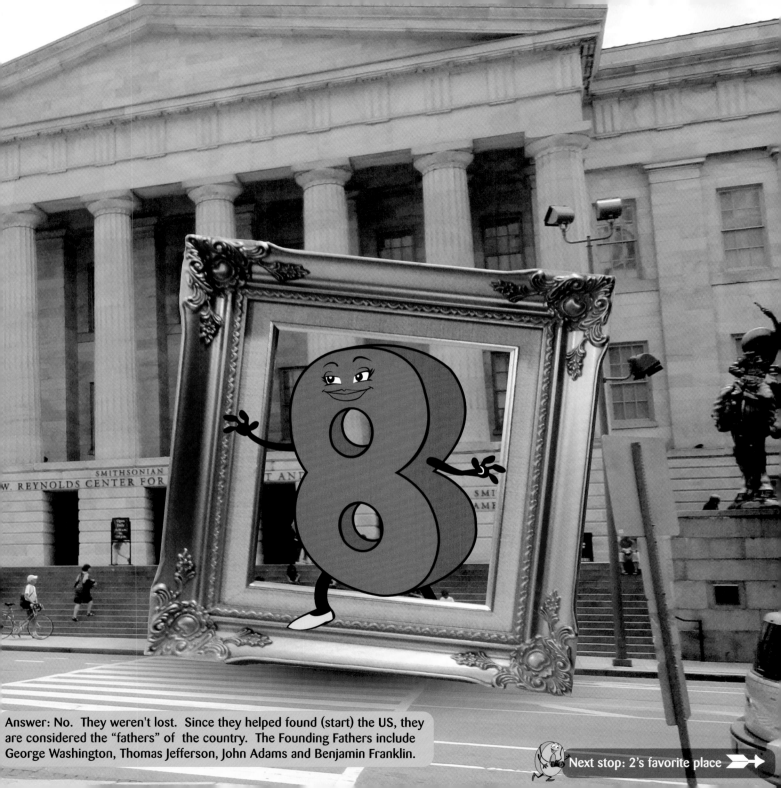

Answer: No. They weren't lost. Since they helped found (start) the US, they are considered the "fathers" of the country. The Founding Fathers include George Washington, Thomas Jefferson, John Adams and Benjamin Franklin.

Next stop: 2's favorite place ➡➡

Answer: Vietnam is in Southeast Asia, more than 8,000 miles from the US.

Next stop: Lincoln Memorial ➤➤

Factoid: A score is an old-fashioned way of saying 20. So "four score and seven years" means 87 years.

The 16th president was a fearless man.

During the Civil War he had a great plan.

His Gettysburg Address was a declaration

That all people are equal in the nation.

FOUR SCORE AND SEVEN YEARS AGO…

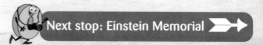
Next stop: Einstein Memorial

Answer: The other speech carved into the wall is Lincoln's 2nd inaugural address.

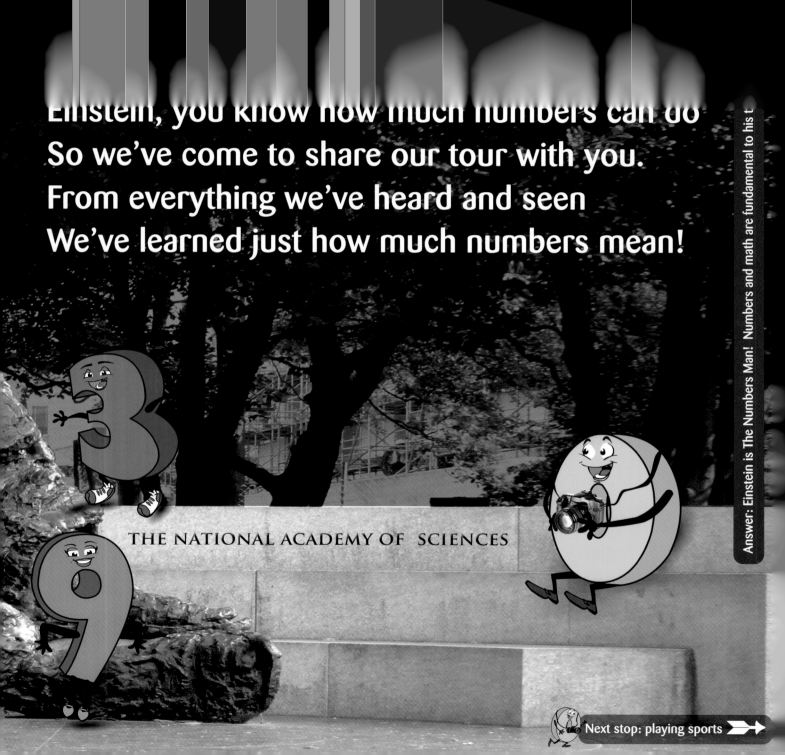

Einstein, you know how much numbers can do
So we've come to share our tour with you.
From everything we've heard and seen
We've learned just how much numbers mean!

THE NATIONAL ACADEMY OF SCIENCES

Answer: Einstein is The Numbers Man! Numbers and math are fundamental to his t

Next stop: playing sports

Team Ten likes fitness and exercise too.
They've biked and walked this tour with you.
Each number feels good by playing a sport
So head to the grass or find the right court!

Why is 7 kicking the football after the touchdown?

Factoid: Washington, DC has 6 professional teams: the Redskins, Nationals, Capitals, DC United, Mystics and Wizards.

 Next stop: Additional places to visit ➡

We hope you liked all the sites on this tour.
We wish we had time to take you to more.
If you stay longer in Washington, DC
Here are other places you may want to see.

Factoid: There are many other fun sights to see in Washington, DC! For example, check out the Natural History Museum and Roosevelt Island.

Thomas Jefferson Memorial

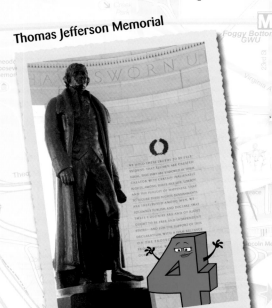

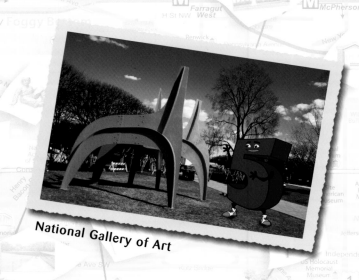

National Gallery of Art

Are all of these locations in the city of Washington, DC?

National Museum of the American Indian

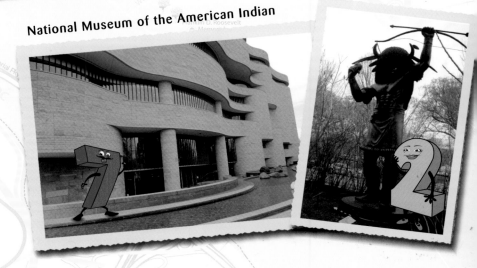

Library of Congress

Arlington National Cemetery

National Zoo

Answer: No. Arlington Cemetery is in Virginia, just across the Potomac River from Washington, DC.

Next page: Fun Facts ⟩⟩

Fun Facts about Washington, DC

Welcome to Washington, DC City Hall

DC stands for the District of Columbia. It is not a state. DC was created from a 10-square mile area of land granted by the states of Maryland and Virginia, but the section from Virginia was returned in 1846. In Roman numerals, DC means 600. The Wilson Building is home to Washington, DC's Mayor and the Council of the District of Columbia. Languages bordering the welcome page are as follows: Top, left to right: Chinese, French, Korean, English, Hindi, German, Arabic; Bottom left to right: Russian, Japanese, Turkish, Spanish.

Location: 1350 Pennsylvania Ave, NW
Closest metro: Federal Triangle
www.dc.gov and www.washington.org

The White House

The White House has been the home of every president except George Washington, although it wasn't called the White House until 1901 (under Theodore Roosevelt). If you hear that a flag out front means the president is home, it is a myth – the flag is flown every day. Visits must be arranged in advance through a member of the US Congress.

Location: 1600 Pennsylvania Ave, NW
Closest metro: McPherson Square; Farragut West
www.whitehouse.gov/about/tours-and-events

Washington Monument

The Washington Monument is 555 feet and 5 $\frac{1}{8}$ inches tall, and from the top you can see for more than 30 miles! The color changes partway up because construction stopped from 1856 to 1876 due to fundraising problems and the Civil War. When it started again, they couldn't find stone of the exact same color as before! An annual kite festival is held in front of the monument. Due to damage from the magnitude 5.8 earthquake of August 2011, the monument was closed to the public. Check the website below for current information.

Location: center of the National Mall
Closest metro: Smithsonian; Federal Triangle
www.nps.gov/wamo

Hirshhorn Museum and Sculpture Garden

The Hirshhorn Museum and Sculpture Garden showcases modern art and sculpture. It has nearly 12,000 paintings, sculptures, photographs, and mixed-media works. When it was built, the building was controversial because its modern style looked so different from the traditional buildings on the Mall.

Location: National Mall at the corner of 7th St and Independence Ave, SW
Closest metro: L'Enfant Plaza; Smithsonian
www.hirshhorn.si.edu

National Air and Space Museum

The Air and Space Museum is DC's most popular museum for kids. The objects pictured in the book are (clockwise from top left): Space Shuttle Discovery, Apollo 11 Command Module "Columbia", Bensen B-6 Gyroglider, Apollo Lunar Module, and the 1903 Wright Flyer. The left page shows a real moon rock that you can touch at the museum. An additional location, the Udvar-Hazy Center – located in northern Virginia near the Washington Dulles International Airport on Interstate 66 – has space for larger rockets, satellites and aircraft, including the space shuttles Enterprise and Discovery.

Location: National Mall at the corner of Independence Ave and 6th St, SW
Closest metro: Smithsonian; L'Enfant Plaza
Additional location: the Udvar-Hazy Center, 14390 Air and Space Museum Parkway, Chantilly, VA
www.nasm.si.edu

US Capitol

The Capitol is the building where the US Senate and the House of Representatives meet. Since it's located on a hill, the neighborhood is called Capitol Hill. Inside, each state has two statues in the National Statuary Hall Collection. The Capitol Visitor Center opened in 2008 and has 580,000 square feet of exhibition halls and meeting space – all underground. The word "capitol"

with an "o" refers to the Capitol Building. Capital is spelled with an "a" in almost all other situations (such as capital letter, capital punishment, capital city).
Location: Visitor Center at 1st and East Capitol Sts, NE (eastern end of the Mall)
Closest metro: Union Station; Capitol South
www.visitthecapitol.gov

US Supreme Court
The Supreme Court building was designed to look like a Greek temple. Here, the 9 Supreme Court Justices interpret the Constitution. In the name of democracy and open government, all Court sessions are open to the public. The Court's motto, inscribed above the columns, is "Equal justice under law."
Location: 1st St between East Capitol St and Maryland Ave, NE
Closest metro: Capitol South; Union Station
www.supremecourt.gov/visiting

The National Mall
The National Mall is a 2-mile-long open green space in the heart of Washington – from the Capitol building to the Lincoln Memorial. It gets 24 million visitors each year. Most of the buildings on the National Mall are part of the Smithsonian Institution, which runs 19 free, public museums. One fun thing to do on the Mall is to visit the Carousel, a 19th century merry-go-round.
Location: center of the city
Closest metro: Smithsonian; L'Enfant Plaza; Archives-Navy Memorial-Penn Quarter
www.nps.gov/mall

Cherry Blossoms around the Tidal Basin
The Tidal Basin is a large man-made lake. It's surrounded by more than 3,000 cherry trees, which were a gift from Japan in 1912. The Jefferson Memorial is across the Tidal Basin from where Team Ten is having lunch. Every spring, Washington, DC welcomes hundreds of thousands of visitors for the Cherry Blossom Festival and parade.
Location: West Potomac Park (south of the Washington Monument)
Closest metro: Smithsonian
www.nps.gov/cherry and
www.nationalcherryblossomfestival.org

Martin Luther King, Jr. Memorial
Martin Luther King, Jr. was a leader of the civil rights movement in the 1950s and 1960s. He used nonviolent methods to fight segregation and encourage equality, peace and justice. His "I Have a Dream" speech, at the end of the March on Washington, was given in front of more than 200,000 people. This is Washington's newest memorial: it was dedicated in 2011.
Location: West Potomac Park (south of the Washington Monument, on the west side of the Tidal Basin)
Closest metro: Smithsonian
www.nps.gov/mlkm and
www.mlkmemorial.org

Washington Metro and Potomac River
The Washington Metro, which opened in 1976, has 5 lines (named for different colors) and 86 stations. It's a convenient way to get around the city, and it also goes to Virginia and Maryland. Be sure to stand on the right when you're on the escalators! The Potomac River runs more than 400 miles from West Virginia to the Chesapeake Bay. It divides DC from Virginia; further north, it divides Maryland and Virginia.
www.wmata.com/rail

The Pentagon
The Pentagon is one of the world's largest buildings, with more than 3.7 million square feet of space. It's so big that it's visible from space – in fact, the image was taken by a GeoEye satellite flying 423 miles above the Earth at 17,000 mph! In addition to its 5 sides, the building also has 5 rings and 5 above-ground floors. But don't expect to see any 5-star generals there, since there are none living. Public tours are limited and must be reserved in advance through the Pentagon website or through a member of Congress.
Location: 1400 Defense Pentagon, Arlington, VA
Closest metro: Pentagon
http://pentagon.afis.osd.mil

More Fun Facts ➤

Fun Facts about Washington, DC

National Archives
The National Archives preserves and provides access to the records of the US government. 3 of the most famous documents you will see are the Declaration of Independence, the Constitution, and the Bill of Rights.
Location: Constitution Ave between 7th and 9th Sts, NW
Closest metro: Archives-Navy Memorial-Penn Quarter
www.archives.gov/nae/visit

Chinatown Friendship Arch
This colorful archway, or "paifang" in Chinese, welcomes visitors to DC's Chinatown. Beijing is one of Washington's sister cities, and the arch's dedication in 1986 was attended by the mayors of both cities.
Location: corner of 7th and H Sts, NW
Closest metro: Gallery Place-Chinatown
No official website

National Portrait Gallery
Here you can find portraits of famous Americans, from political leaders like George Washington to artists like Mary Cassatt and pop figures like Marilyn Monroe. The Portrait Gallery shares the building with another museum, the American Art Museum. Be sure to check out the covered courtyard in the middle, with its wavy modern glass roof!
Location: 8th and F Sts, NW
Closest metro: Gallery Place-Chinatown
www.npg.si.edu

Vietnam Veterans Memorial and Vietnam Women's Memorial
Architect Maya Lin's moving Vietnam Veterans Memorial focuses attention on the names of those who died in the Vietnam War. The 2 walls point to the Washington Monument and the Lincoln Memorial. Each wall is 246.75 feet long, and together they have more than 58,000 names inscribed in chronological order by the date of casualty. There is also a Vietnam Women's Memorial honoring the women who served in the war.
Location: West Potomac Park (western end of the Mall)
Closest metro: Foggy Bottom-GWU
www.nps.gov/vive

Lincoln Memorial
Construction of the Lincoln Memorial began in 1914 to celebrate the 16th US President; the dedication took place in 1922. The words of his Gettysburg Address and 2nd inaugural address are carved on the walls of the Lincoln Memorial. There are 98 steps from the Reflecting Pool to the Lincoln Memorial.
Location: West Potomac Park (western end of the Mall)
Closest metro: Foggy Bottom-GWU
www.nps.gov/linc

Einstein Memorial
Albert Einstein is considered the father of physics – he's 'The Numbers Man'! He was born in Germany but immigrated to the United States in 1933. This memorial is on the grounds of the National Academy of Sciences and was unveiled in 1979, in honor of Einstein's 100th birthday.
Location: Constitution Avenue and 22nd St, NW (across from the Vietnam Veterans Memorial)
Closest metro: Foggy Bottom-GWU
www.nasonline.org/about-nas/visiting-nas/nas-building/the-einstein-memorial.html

Sports

There's a reason why the numbers picked the sports they're playing! 6 likes ice hockey because there are 6 people on a team. 1 likes the shape of the baseball bat, and 4 loves running around the 4 bases shaped like a diamond. In basketball, each basket earns 2 or 3 points – so 2 and 3 are hoping for a basket! 5 loves that the soccer ball is made up of pentagons, and goalie 8 guards the goal that is 8 feet tall. The ancient Mayan 0 was a pointed oval, similar to the shape of a football. 7 is getting ready to kick the football in hopes of earning the extra (7th) point after a touchdown. Last but not least is 9, who is a cheerleader because she loves being "dressed to the nines," as they say!

Washington has six professional sports teams:

Redskins (football):
www.redskins.com

DC United (soccer):
www.dcunited.com

Capitals (ice hockey):
http://capitals.nhl.com

Wizards (men's basketball):
www.nba.com/wizards

Mystics (women's basketball):
www.wnba.com/mystics

Nationals (baseball):
http://washington.nationals.mlb.com

OTHER LOCATIONS OF INTEREST

National Gallery of Art.
The National Gallery is one of the nation's great art museums. The West building has traditional art, and the geometric East Building has modern art. In between, the underground passage showcases a cascading fountain. Be sure to check out the cool sculptures in the Sculpture Garden, including the red Calder horse in the photo. **www.nga.gov**

Thomas Jefferson Memorial.
Thomas Jefferson was the 3rd president and is most famous for drafting the Declaration of Independence in 1776. The memorial is modeled after Rome's Pantheon. The statue is made of bronze and measures 19 feet tall. **www.nps.gov/thje**

National Museum of the American Indian.
This is the newest museum on the National Mall, opening in 2004. The wavy building is made of limestone and designed to evoke connections with nature. **www.nmai.si.edu**

Library of Congress.
This is the largest library in the world, with more than 151 million items. The main reading room has a magnificent dome that's 160 feet tall. **www.loc.gov**

Arlington National Cemetery.
This is the burial grounds of many US heroes, including President John F. Kennedy and hundreds of thousands of military veterans. Each day at the Tomb of the Unknown Soldier, there are regular, public ceremonies to honor the men and women of the military. **www.arlingtoncemetery.mil**

National Zoo.
At the National Zoo, you can visit more than 2,000 animals of 400 species. The zoo's 2 most well-known residents are the giant pandas named Mei Xiang and Tian Tian. **www.nationalzoo.si.edu**

LAST STOP

Ronald Reagan Washington National Airport
This is just 1 of 3 airports near Washington – but none of them is actually in Washington, DC! Reagan National and Dulles International are in Virginia, and Baltimore-Washington International is in Maryland.

Location: 1 Aviation Circle, Arlington, VA
Closest metro: Ronald Reagan Washington National Airport
www.metwashairports.com/reagan

Next stop: Reagan National Airport ⟩⟩

Guide for Parents and Teachers

NumbersAlive! Books for Young Travelers involve real-world educational quests for pre-K through Grade 5 children, accompanied on their journeys by parents, teachers, librarians, or other caring adults. The books encourage children to understand and identify numbers and relate them to applications in their own surroundings at a formative early-childhood stage of learning. Accurate observation, analysis, and creative thinking form the basis of exploration and the scientific method. Children will discover applied numbers and mathematics and learn that they are tools that we use to understand, describe, and improve our world.

Dr. Klemm believes that friendly, fun, and interactive daily experiences with numbers will encourage understanding of applied numbers and establish a solid foundation for math skills. Discovering how numbers are used in actual environments as shapes, quantities, names, and order sequences reinforces the relevance of applied numbers. Observing and discussing numerical applications are critical steps to math literacy. Daily activities become the laboratory of learning and form a solid foundation for more abstract concepts.

Your children will enjoy *NumbersAlive! Books for Young Travelers:*

Washington, DC at home and while visiting the capital. If the children are in the pre-K age range, they will like the pictures and rhythm of the verses. They will begin to identify locations in Washington, DC while they learn their numbers and appreciate their relevance by observing them in the locations. As children mature, they will develop higher-order thinking as they discover more details on each of the pages, respond to the questions, and understand the factoids. They may also be inspired to work alone or with help to investigate the DC locations further by using the web sites provided on the "Fun Facts" pages or look for additional number and mathematical patterns hidden in the book.

Your book is a starting point to learn more about US history and culture. Each page highlights a location with specific educational references ranging from the Revolutionary War (Washington Monument) to the Civil Rights Movement (Martin Luther King, Jr. Memorial).

Your book can be used to plan a personal tour of Washington, DC with Team Ten. Encourage your children to choose location(s) they want to explore. Older children can use the map to help plan the itinerary. While in Washington, DC, encourage children to take their own photos of the locations visited and see how many additional number applications they can identify.

At home or in the classroom, the book can be used as the basis for numerical explorations in the children's own environment. Start by having them search for number applications in their home, classroom, or city. They may also identify different ways in which numbers appear:

- Quantity or counting, such as the 8 columns of the National Portrait Gallery.
- Shape, such as the triangle at the top of the National Archives.
- Name, such as the Chinatown Friendship Archway on 7th Street.
- Order and sequence, such at the 1st president in the rhyme about the Washington Monument.

See what number applications your children can identify, and have them draw the number shapes or quantities that they find in their own environment. Older children can plan a personal Team Ten tour by simply choosing a location or object to demonstrate the relevance of each number.

Please send us your ideas, suggestions, and thoughts about *Numbers Alive! Books for Young Travelers: Washington, DC.*